ACCELERATE

20 High Performance Questions to Supercharge Your Business

PATRICK BURKE

BEACON

Also by Patrick Burke

Exit Velocity
Swing for the Fences

Cover design: Snap Advertising
Interior: Madeline Harris

ISBN: 978-1-929266-79-1 (hardcover)

Printed in the United States of America

For my children:

Meggie, Jake, and Ellie,
whose many questions spawned a million invaluable insights

CONTENTS

PREFACE

My phone buzzed and my assistant, Dianne, announced, "It's Mark from Big M Tool and Die." I picked up the phone, and Mark characteristically started talking without a salutation. "My business broker tells me I'm going to receive an offer on my business today. I'm hoping for 1.2 million—any advice?"

"No," I replied while thinking, *Too late*. "I'll review it for you if you'd like."

"Thanks. I am really looking forward to some R & R."

As I hung up I recalled a meeting with Mark two months earlier, in which he'd told me he was completely burned out and needed to sell his business now. I also remember telling him that based on his company's low score on the 20 High-Performance Questions, he needed to spend significant time with me working on his business rather than *in* it.

The next day Mark called again. "I got my offer," he said flatly. "It's only six hundred thousand, and the buyer wants me to stay on for a year since she doesn't believe my company's performance is sustainable unless I'm here every day. If I am going to hang on that long, maybe it's time I got after your 20 Questions."

I responded, "You're right, Mark. Let's get started immediately."

As a strategic advisor, CPA, and attorney I have had the pleasure of working shoulder-to-shoulder with hundreds of business owners like Mark. Throughout my thirty-five years of experience, I've noticed that some businesses merely survive and provide the owner with a job, while others thrive, not only generating huge profits but also becoming extremely valuable assets. The owners of the thriving businesses are no smarter than the owners of the surviving businesses, and their products or services are not necessarily better. So what sets them apart?

In response to that question, I analyzed my most successful clients and developed a 360-degree process that improves not only the profitability of a business but also its transferable value. For this book I distilled the process into the 20 most important questions business owners must answer about themselves and their businesses. You will correctly identify yourself and your business if you answer the questions honestly. Warning: You will likely be disappointed with the result.

Whether it's through a sale or a gift/inheritance, a business must either transition or die. Unfortunately only 10 percent of businesses sell or make it to a third generation. With so many underemployed millennials, buyers looking for investments, and unemployed folks looking to create their own jobs, why are the odds of a successful transition so low? In my opinion it's because most often the owner is the business. This is true not only of professional practices in which the owner is the only income producer but also of operating companies with owners who have allowed themselves to become indispensable. As a business owner, you must focus on two disparate aspects of your business in order for it to thrive. First are the aspects at which you excel. These aspects must be magnified through systems that allow others to match your excellence. Second are those aspects at which you're weakest and therefore least interested in.

Your weaknesses must be carefully scrutinized to ensure your disinterest has not resulted in their ineffectiveness, retooled if necessary to make certain they work, and finally systemized to maximize their value to your company.

Most business owners fail to make the journey from profitable to valuable because they don't know the route and they're unwilling to pay someone who does. I love guiding business owners on this journey because it not only leads to maximizing the profits and value of their current business but also reignites their entrepreneurial spirit, motivating them to hit the next level of performance or maybe even start a new enterprise. So hit the accelerator and let's go!

HOW TO READ THIS BOOK

Each of the 20 High-Performance Questions has three possible answers. Choose the answer that most closely matches your company. The scoring is explained at the end of the book where you'll find out how you and your business stack up. Use this book as a scorecard to see which areas of your business need improvement. I also encourage you to use it as a workbook and mark up the pages with ideas as you consider how you can improve the performance of your business.

1. DOES YOUR SALES FORECAST PREDICT A PROLONGED DRY SPELL?

A.   Our sales referral network is something I carefully nurtured throughout my career. I guard it like the Hope Diamond. As a result, I do practically all the prospecting, lead generation, and sales calls. I also close most of our deals. It seems I have lost a step since our sales growth has stalled. I have thought about turning at least part of my process over to others within the organization, but because I don't recruit with sales in mind, I don't have the right people. I am successful at sales because I simply know how to encourage customers to like me, and in the end people do business with their friends.

B.   I have a couple of salespeople who occasionally unearth a lead like a blind squirrel finds an acorn. They even close a deal here and there, but they sell primarily on price, not value. I really can't articulate their game plan, and I am confident they can't either.

C.   Our crack sales team systematically, regularly, and successfully prospects and originates killer sales leads and closes deals. Its processes are well documented and easy to follow, making adding and training new team members a snap. We start them out as business development associates making phone calls to prospects. We find that this somewhat grueling self-selection process is a great way to source the next outside sales superstar.

Like most business owners, you likely started off as your company's only salesperson. Over time, either through inspiration or perspiration born of absolute necessity, you developed successful sales techniques. Despite what you may think, these techniques can be learned and eventually mastered by others, thus creating an effective sales team.

By documenting and utilizing effective sales processes, you can transform your sales team members into rainmakers. The dance required to make it rain may not be *Swan Lake*, but neither is it the Twist, and although it may not seem like it, it can be reduced to a series of steps. It may be that your sales team is not able to dance like Gene Kelly; however, by following the right sales processes, they can still make it rain.

NOTES

NOTES

2. WHEN WAS THE LAST TIME YOUR PRODUCTS OR SERVICES TESTED THE FREE AGENCY MARKET?

A.   We price our products to yield the same gross profit percentage every year. We increase prices only in response to dramatic increases in our costs. I have no idea what the market will bear or how our value is perceived by our customers or the marketplace.

B.   We occasionally check out our competitors' prices and make minor upticks when we're absolutely sure our customers will accept the increase. We don't do this with any consistency, so these minor increases don't increase earnings regularly.

C.   We not only monitor costs and conduct competitive analyses, we also regularly seek feedback from our customers on how we are doing and what we could do to be more valuable to them. As a result I know when we have pricing power, and I'm not afraid to leverage this advantage.

Proper pricing is possible only if you truly understand your products' points of differentiation and your customers' perception of the resultant increase in marginal value.

You don't necessarily need high-end qualitative market research to find this out. Hiring a marketing firm to administer a simple survey will provide a good start for what should be an ongoing process.

We all know the story of the hometown hero. He spends a long career with the home team and decides after an offer that he perceives as penurious to test the free agency market and *bam*—he lands a huge new contract with a team that perennially competes for the championship. Don't let your product or service languish in hometown purgatory. Figure out its true worth and charge accordingly.

NOTES

NOTES

3. ARE YOU KEEPING UP WITH THE JONESES OR LOOKING INTO THEIR BASEMENT WINDOW?

A. We do business like we always have. As far as we're concerned, we don't have any real competition. Our sales slowdown and margin erosion are inevitable by-products of a tough economy. The products and services we offer never change. I believe consistency is a virtue, and our client base is mostly loyal. However, I must admit they are aging and pulling in their horns a bit.

B. From time to time, we alter our offerings, particularly when we see a competitor being successful with something new. These new products have occasionally led to new opportunities with current customers but rarely to any new customers.

C. I watch our market like an NSA analyst. Not only do I know what our competition is offering, I also know their target markets, pricing, and sales pitch. When I see a good idea, we copy it, improve it, and then charge more for it. As a result we consistently win profitable new business from our competitors' customers, which fuels above-market growth and profitability.

You want to believe your products are best-of-class and that both your current and prospective customers are happy to buy from your company at premium prices. However, without empirical evidence you really can't know if you are keeping up with the Joneses. The Joneses didn't end up living in the McMansion on Big Bucks Boulevard by chance. They know your people and products better than you do and are calling on your customers right now with a product offering you don't have yet. Getting essential intelligence on the Joneses will take more than smudging their basement window with your nose. Get serious—fly your drone over their new product lawn party and beat them to the market with your own superior product. Much of what you need to know about your competition is readily available on their website. Get snooping!

NOTES

NOTES

4. THE LAST TIME YOU HAD A DISPUTE WITH AN EMPLOYEE, DID YOU END UP WITH THE BLACK EYE?

A.   When it comes to dealing with our employees, my motto is flexibility. I believe every situation must be addressed, taking into consideration any number of external factors, including the employee's tenure with the company, the company's current financial situation, as well as the difficulty of replacing the employee. Although this ad-hocracy causes a few problems, including more than a couple of sizable bills from our labor lawyer, I continue to believe our King Solomon–esque wisdom correctly solves most employee issues.

B.   We have committed some employee policies to writing in a document that is not quite an employee manual. These policies prevent our HR department from getting into as many disputes as it did before. Employees likely believe the company handles matters more or less evenhandedly. Frankly, it is much better than it was.

C.   We work very hard to spell out our company's employment policies in an easy-to-understand employee manual. We spent the time to put this manual together because I realize most employment-related issues end up in a jump ball, which the company generally loses. Now I believe the certainty of our vacation, overtime, benefits, and promotion policies is a contributing factor to not only attracting the best talent but also retaining it. Our HR folks spend most of their time training and keeping up with benefit trends and changes in the employment laws. I truly believe our HR department has gone from being a significant cost center to being one of the principal reasons for our industry-leading profit margins.

I have never met an entrepreneur who enjoys dealing with employee problems. You likely view such issues as gripes and maybe even a tad disloyal; certainly you see them as evidence of a lack of the hustle one needs to succeed. Removing all subjectivity from this key area and adopting progressive policies (think flextime) is an essential factor in keeping topflight performers and ensuring topflight results.

NOTES

NOTES

5. DO YOUR FINANCIAL STATEMENTS LOOK MORE LIKE THE TOP LINE ON THE EYE CHART OR THE LEAVES AT THE BOTTOM OF A TEACUP?

A. I can gauge my company's performance by the jingle in my jeans. I don't really use my financial statements for much of anything except to send to my accountant for my annual taxes. I have tried from time to time to expand my business by borrowing money from the bank, but the loan officers don't seem to think my financial statements are accurate. I'll have to admit I agree with them. I'm sure the company is doing much better than the statements indicate, but isn't that just good tax planning? Clearly our bookkeeping department is nothing but a cost center.

B. I spend some time analyzing our income statement to see if we are making enough money. I also occasionally check out our gross profit to make sure we're monitoring costs. Our balance sheet is really just a dustcover for our income statement. Although the balance sheet doesn't mean much to me, I know our bank scrutinizes it pretty carefully, particularly when we are trying to dial up our credit line or borrow money to buy new equipment. The company is often turned down because the bank believes we are what they call "over-leveraged." I have always taken as much money as possible out of the business; after all, I earned it and have significant personal financial needs.

C.   I carefully monitor our financial results, know our industry's key financial performance indicators, and strive to meet or exceed them every month. I charge management with maintaining their teams' metrics and expect them to hit their numbers. I believe our accounting department's scrutiny and oversight ensures excellent performance and is a key element of our growth engine. Our bank loves us. We are never turned down when we ask for additional financing. Each year we drop a higher portion of sales to the bottom line than in the previous year.

Although painful, to be a successful business owner, you must have accurate and timely financial information and truly know how to interpret it. Monitoring this data doesn't mean occasionally checking your score. The most successful owners use financial information to fine-tune operations, evaluate personnel, manage vendors, and, most important, drive profits and sustainable growth.

NOTES

NOTES

6. HOW LONG IS YOUR END OF THE VENDOR STICK?

A. We are extremely loyal to our vendors and are very proud of our long association with this tight-knit group. I will admit, from time to time, some vendors fall short of our expectations. Maybe they misinterpret our loyalty as complete satisfaction with their products, services, and pricing. We are pretty timid about testing the market. I suppose the inertia is due to fear of the unknown and the hassle of breaking in someone new.

B. We try to maintain our vendor team, but when I sense complacency, as evidenced by an unannounced price increase or a drop-off in the level of service, I am fairly vocal about it. This usually results in improved pricing or responsiveness. On the rare occasion when we fire a vendor, we find that our new ones are only slightly better than their predecessors.

C. We constantly monitor our vendor relations. We pay on time every month, thus holding up our end of the bargain, so we insist that our vendors hold up theirs. Even if our relationship with a vendor is good, I carefully monitor the marketplace and will take calls and meet with potential new vendors. Our vendors know this, and it keeps them on their toes. However, if we find someone new who is offering better pricing or a higher level of service, we always give the incumbent a chance to match it. I believe this is the appropriate level of loyalty. Honestly, some of our best vendors are those who have experienced this crucible. We are not necessarily price shoppers, but we demand—and believe we receive—value from our vendors commensurate with price.

If you are not actively and regularly evaluating your vendor team, you are definitely getting the short end of the stick. Your purchasing agent, office manager, or general manager should be tasked with evaluating vendors every year or two. If you have never done this before, it may initially feel like you are being disloyal, but just like in your relationship with your customers, you much prefer being kept on your toes to being cut off at the knees.

NOTES

NOTES

7. IS YOUR COMPENSATION SYSTEM ELEVATING YOUR EMPLOYEE'S GAME OR ARE YOUR EMPLOYEES GAMING THE SYSTEM?

A.   Our compensation and bonus plans are based largely on longevity. Occasionally we will go out of our pay bands to replace one of our more senior personnel. We haven't recently had our pay scale marked to market, but I would guess we're higher than average on our longest-term employees, due primarily to social promotion. Honestly, I believe that our high fixed employee cost is the primary reason our margins are shrinking. Moreover, our compensation levels leave little room to pay exceptional employees higher wages.

B.   We have successfully broken out of locking compensation levels primarily to years of service. I believe we know which employees are delivering extraordinary performance, and we are fattening their pay envelopes appropriately. However, if we plot our employment-related costs over time, the costs will vary based more upon the age and longevity of our employees than on actual company performance. We added an objective component or two to our compensation plan, but I still believe rewarding employees based on subjective standards such as attitude and esprit de corps is important.

C.   We consider our base compensation and bonus plans to be one of the principal reasons we are able to attract and retain top talent. We set objective goals for all employees; their compensation is based upon attaining these goals. As a result, our employee costs are far more variable, which results in not only lower costs in lean times but also flexibility to pay up for extraordinary talent.

Your compensation system should incentivize employees and elevate their game to the highest level as determined by the goals they have mutually agreed upon with company management. Systems that predicate base pay on tenure and bonus pay on subjective standards encourage employees to simply game the system and not excel. Well thought-out compensation systems linked directly to employee performance metrics are essential to building a team that wins new business, creates efficient operations, develops new ideas, and builds durable value for your company.

NOTES

NOTES

8. IS BETTING THE RANCH HOW YOU RUN YOUR RANCH?

A. In all respects I run my business conservatively. I don't see a strong need to guard against risk because my company doesn't engage in risky practices. I believe I'm an excellent judge of character and hire only those I know to be of the highest moral fiber. As a result, I spend little time worrying about employee dishonesty and even less time with our insurance agent discussing our practically nonexistent liability or loss exposure. I am not worried because we have never been sued or stolen from (as far as I know).

B. I am generally aware of the need to manage risk. I have our CPAs look at our books periodically, and they never mention any indication of employee dishonesty. I see our insurance agent each year and discuss in broad terms what he believes to be our most significant exposures. He routinely states we are underinsured, but then again, he's really just a salesman; that's his job.

C. Protecting the valuable asset our team has built is of paramount importance. Our CFO considers risk management one of her key roles. I believe our process-es, including our strong internal controls and careful alignment of customers' expectations to our products' performance, are strong guards against losses and litigation. I have a great relationship with our insur-ance agent, who carefully specifies our exposures, how to mitigate them, and the appropriate coverages, which include significant umbrella coverage.

As an entrepreneur you are likely a risk taker by nature, which is generally a positive for your business. This is particularly true as it relates to you dreaming up, starting, and funding new business lines. However, this "bet the ranch" outlook combined with a "let's go" skill set are liabilities when risk management is the goal. Building real value in your company means deploying processes to minimize losses and fully insuring against risks that are beyond your control.

NOTES

NOTES

9. IF YOUR BUDGET WERE A MOVIE, WOULD IT BE *GROUNDHOG DAY* OR *2001: A SPACE ODYSSEY*?

A.   My budget process is quite simple. I take the prior year's actual results and add or subtract a percentage point or so, depending on my take on our marketplace as well as the economy. I rarely involve team members other than our controller, who creates the spreadsheet. I occasionally compare our actual results to our budget, but that has usually proven meaningless. Honestly, the best thing I can say about our budget is that it is consistent—as in consistently wrong. We fail to predict any uptick or downtick. As a result, no one trusts or uses it for planning or goal setting.

B.   Based on some industry information I may have heard at a conference, I will tweak our prior year's results to create the budget. Exactly how that information will affect sales and profits is based largely on Kentucky windage. That being said, I have been on target maybe 25 percent of the time. Although that makes me feel smarter in those years, I can't say our process is refined to the point that meaningful individual or company performance goals can be set. I must admit our budget is an interesting undertaking, but as a management tool it's ineffective.

C.   Our budget is our primary business-management tool. We start the process with a blank slate. After receiving a detailed sales forecast based on our sales department's pipeline, we carefully build our cost estimates. Because of our faith in our sales numbers, we can accurately predict our costs and often negotiate better prices with our vendors based on our willingness to order early. Our budget also sets the minimum employee productivity goals, which we use to set our base compensation levels as well as bonus targets. Because we have been spot-on in our predictions, our bank has worked with us to facilitate our growth by providing timely increases in our line of credit. I couldn't run my company at anywhere close to its current high level of profitability without our budget.

Most business owners believe they can't accurately predict next year's performance; as a result, they prepare a budget based almost solely on the prior year (the *Groundhog Day* approach) or prepare no budget at all. Accurately predicting the future, like *2001: A Space Odyssey*, can be accomplished if you are willing to spend time to understand your products' place in the market as well as the business environment and how they interact to affect your company's future performance. As Yogi Berra said, "If you don't know where you are going, you might wind up someplace else."

NOTES

NOTES

10. DOES YOUR BANKER BUY YOUR VISION OR JUST AN OCCASIONAL LUNCH?

A.   When it comes to bankers—and banks, for that matter—I really can't afford to be picky. The company borrows money from just about any bank (and there aren't many) that agrees to lend it to us. Since we don't prepare a strategic growth plan or budget, we have little to share with bankers when we run short on capital. On the rare occasion we receive more than one proposal, we choose a bank based strictly upon price and terms.

B.   Although our banker is not part of my inner circle of advisers, we have a friendly relationship. In the past, when times were tougher, the relationship with our banker was somewhat contentious. Now that we are more financially secure, I am confident in sharing our long-term goals. I can't say she truly gets where we are going, but then again, my GPS has led me into more than a few culs-de-sac. Because our past performance is checkered, I don't believe we have the clout to negotiate hard when we are looking to renew our bank facility.

C.   I spend the time necessary to fully educate our banker on our long-term plans. I even seek his strategic input because he has serviced larger, more successful companies than ours. Because he is part of our decision-making team and we understand what the bank requires in terms of growth, profits, and equity, we always receive timely commitments and fair terms when we need debt to grow. I believe that because of my considerable interaction with our banker, I have a clear understanding of the underwriting process and standards. As a result, we are not shy about issuing RFPs to other banks, but in the end I believe a strong relationship is more important than price and terms (within reason!).

To share a vision, you must first have one. Bringing your banker into your confidence and having him or her buy into your vision is critical. No matter how great your company's success, access to capital on advantageous terms will always be necessary to fuel growth. It is likely that the tightening of bank margins and consolidation of the industry is making your banker less accessible. However, it's worth what may be a significant effort to develop and nurture an "inside the circle" relationship with your banker.

NOTES

NOTES

11. HOW CLOSE TOGETHER ARE YOUR COMPANY'S PENCIL MARKS ON THE KITCHEN DOORWAY?

A.   Our growth pattern pretty much mimics economic cycles. However, in some down years we have been able to make lemonade out of lemons, and in some strong economic years, the rising tide hasn't been high enough to get us above our (self-imposed) sandbar. I have the desire to grow, but honestly I am beginning to believe that flat is the new up. Our customer attrition rate exceeds our acquisition rate, and sales growth occurs only when we cut prices. Frankly, I'm afraid this pattern is irreversible, a sentiment that is rippling through our workforce, causing a few key defections.

B.   I monitor our marketplace sporadically. The intelligence I've gathered indicates that the company's fortunes for the most part match our industry. We occasionally gain sales through the introduction of new products and by entering new markets. However, we don't have a process that pushes us to the leading edge in either growth area. We would likely be classified as a market follower, not a leader. We are keeping our doors open, but we are not achieving our full growth potential.

C.   Every year, our management team gets together and outlines a detailed growth plan. Upon completion we do a thorough analysis of our available resources and make additions where necessary. The plan is promulgated company-wide and all personnel know their role and are rewarded when we achieve our goal. Surprisingly, many of our new products and services, as well as new customers, have come from our rank and file. I believe employees having a real investment in our success is essential for its realization.

Your parents likely monitored and recorded your growth by marking your height each year on the kitchen doorway. Some years the pencil marks were so close they almost touched; others were inches apart. Similarly, your company's growth is not assured; rather, it must be carefully planned. The best companies build a strategic growth plan each year before they begin their budget process. The best plans are extremely specific, detailing new products and markets along with the sales approach needed to create demand. This ensures that the planned growth will be supported by adequate physical and human resources and, of course, capital.

NOTES

NOTES

12. DOES MOST OF YOUR ADVICE COME FROM AN ECHO CHAMBER?

A. I make most of my company's big decisions. Keeping my own counsel ensures decisions are made quickly. My motto could be "Ready, fire, aim." In retrospect I admit some of my calls were ill-advised, but I believe doing something is almost always better than doing nothing. On the rare occasions when I solicit advice, I find that my CPA, lawyer, and management team usually agree with me. As a result, I see no need to slow down just for what I view as a rubber stamp.

B. Although I don't have a formal policy for soliciting advice, I have an informal kitchen cabinet. This group includes my CPA and a good friend who is an experienced business operator. I usually contact them when I am in a particularly challenging situation. Their advice is helpful as a one-off, but I can't say it helps us grow or become more profitable, or even that it prevents the next problem. Admittedly, what they know about my company is limited because they are not involved on a regular basis. I should probably keep them more informed so I can receive better advice.

C.   One day it hit me that I was running the biggest company I had ever run and could use some help. I also realized I was afraid to hear anything I didn't already know, and it was limiting my company's growth. As a result, I formed a board of advisers and meet with them quarterly. Not only does their advice help me grow my business faster, but both my team and I benefit greatly from the extensive preparation for each meeting and the inevitable tough questions from the advisers. I really believe my board is one of the primary reasons my company has doubled its growth rate and done it profitably.

It's easy to breathe only your own air. Prying the lid off your business and shedding some antiseptic light on your operations via a board is a tough step to take. A board performs three essential functions: 1) it provides strategic direction and accompanying goals; 2) it suggests effective tactics for accomplishing the goals; and 3) it establishes appropriate corporate governance. Advisers are not micromanagers; their advice is more directional than specific, and it follows the NIFO rule (Nose In, Fingers Out). Pull yourself out of your echo chamber and subject yourself to some advice (I know this is the tough part) from folks who know more than you and are willing to point that out in a blunt but helpful way.

NOTES

NOTES

13. HOW DID YOUR COMPANY DO ON ITS BOARD SCORES?

A. My company is so unique, it is hard to find comparables. As a result, I can only compare our results with those from a prior year or against some very broad industry information. Occasionally these comparisons yield pertinent information, but I can't say it's overly helpful in achieving profitable growth. I believe I am pretty good at dead reckoning and need only a few waypoints to ensure we are headed in the right direction. However, I admit our results don't always look like it.

B. I am fairly active in my industry's trade group and have a rough estimate of how others in the industry are doing. Our trade group publishes standards for sales growth and gross profit percentage, but I am not sure how scientific they are. Moreover, because my company is unique, I am sure it's not a spot-on representation of the industry profile, which, in my opinion, makes using any of the standards suspect.

C. My management team and I run the company to consistently meet or exceed our industry's key performance indicators (KPIs). We're convinced that a significant contributor to our success is the consistent comparing of our results with similar-size companies within our industry. We use KPIs to set performance goals for production, sales, and administrative departments. Further, we tie our employee bonus pay to achieving these goals. We use this valuable information to manage costs and spur sales and production, which results in a higher net income margin every year.

It seems everyone hates standardized tests, from the Iowas to the SATs. Many believe the results reflect only the ability to take tests. However, business statistics, such as the KPIs published by every trade group, are in fact statistically valid indicators of how companies in your industry are performing, including those with best-of-class results (where you want to be, of course). Using industry KPIs and developing your own will establish the dashboard that will have you tracking toward operational excellence.

NOTES

NOTES

14. DOES YOUR ORGANIZATIONAL STRUCTURE LOOK MORE LIKE A PYRAMID OR AN HOURGLASS?

A. I can't really tell you what our organizational chart looks like because we don't have one. I'm in charge of production and sales, and I have the final say in administration, even though I don't technically run it (the bean counters do). I consider anything or anyone that comes between me and a decision to be a waste of valuable time. As my business has grown, I have less time to devote to my greatest strength: sales. Much too often I'm in meetings I find boring and, I believe, too far removed from our primary function for me to remain focused. As a result, I often make a bad decision, which means I waste even more time on the same issue later. It's a cycle that's sapping my entrepreneurial juices. . . . Maybe it's time to sell.

B. Sales, production, and administration each have a department head who reports to me, but I still make 99 percent of the decisions. Although I am the straw that stirs the drink, I have to admit that overreliance on my input results in significant dilution of that drink. Like most entrepreneurs (and predators), I have only two lenses: wide-angle to identify opportunities or threats, and microscopic for kill or be killed. I have neither the capacity nor the desire to focus on the middle ground. I must also admit, our current structure has not resulted in consistent growth or steady profits. I am convinced my strong personality and need for control is making my company weaker.

C.   I know strategy is my strength, but tactics are my weakness. I read *The E Myth* and know successful businesses need middle management. My middle managers have created an effective organizational structure that is based on direction and purpose and insures strategic and effective execution. My business was once organized around personalities (principally mine) but is now operated solely on processes. The change has energized me and my team and has allowed us to achieve outstanding growth and increased profitability year over year.

Like most entrepreneurs, you likely structure your businesses as an hourglass. The large top is you, the entrepreneur, with a big personality and an ego to match—large and in charge. The narrow middle signifies the typical lack of middle management. The large bottom of the hourglass is indicative of the "help." This structure works until you run out of capacity; then something gives. The usual result is that all aspects of your business suffer, including the one aspect that made it a success in the first place (generally some sort of specialized production or perhaps a unique sales proposition). Structuring your business like a big company pyramid may at first seem unnecessarily cumbersome, but over time you'll understand that the middle ground, between the owner and opportunity and threats, is where businesses are successfully operated and grown.

NOTES

NOTES

15. DO YOU ONLY GO SHOPPING WHEN YOU ARE HUNGRY?

A.   We make most of our capital expenditures in response to a current need. Usually it's due to a big order from a good customer we're unable to fulfill without a new piece of equipment. Honestly, I'm not sure it has always been worth it because the equipment is often idle as soon as the project concludes. When we have a good year, we buy equipment I believe we may need. Our banker often declines our loan requests because she thinks we are not disciplined in how we approach our capital expenditures. As a result, we're often required to drain our cash reserves to buy equipment, or to lease it on unattractive terms.

B.   On the rare occasion when we prepare a budget, we sometimes note a mismatch between our sales plan and our capital resources. In those cases, we buy what we believe we'll need to hit our goal. I would say we are right most of the time, but we have a warehouse half full of very serviceable equipment we don't use enough to keep on the floor. Occasionally we fire-sale some items, particularly if our accountant tells us we could use the tax loss or if we need to raise some cash fast.

C.   We prepare our capital expenditures (CAPX) budget along with our operating budget as part of our yearly enterprise-wide resource planning. No item is purchased unless we can prove the return on the investment exceeds our hurdle rate of 15 percent. Because of our stringent standards, our return on invested capital is consistently high, which thrills our bank. Consequently, we're able to borrow to fund our CAPX on great terms. We religiously honor our financial mantra of using short-term debt to fund short-term assets and long-term debt to fund long-term assets. I am very proud of our pristine balance sheet.

Just like hitting the grocery store with no list right before dinner, buying capital assets in response to an immediate need is a poor idea. Although it may seem antithetical to your instincts, not all growth is good. Poor planning yields poor utilization, poor financing options, and poor returns. CAPX budgets that mesh with your operating budget ensure good returns, which will result in favorable financing options, which facilitate good growth.

NOTES

NOTES

16. IS YOUR FAVORITE ENTREPRENEURIAL ANIMAL A WHITE ELEPHANT OR A CASH COW?

A. I hear from friends there are plenty of people looking to buy good companies, so I'm confident that when the time comes for me to move on, my company will be salable at a good price. It provides a great living for me, and I am sure the next owner, like me, will have enough lucky breaks to also be successful. He or she will need to be a lot like me, a jack-of-all-trades as well as a shrewd risk taker. I believe that fits the profile of most serious buyers.

B. Although my company is successful, I know my input is our principal advantage. However, I have recently brought a few of my team members into my confidence so that I am not as critical to our success as I once was. None of the folks know the whole picture, but I would say together they have the principal pieces of the puzzle covered. This group could either band together to buy me out or be an adequate management team for a new buyer. Honestly, running my company is so consumptive, "What's next?" is clearly a back-burner issue.

C.   I run my company so it could be sold tomorrow for top dollar. If you looked up *process-driven* in the dictionary, you would see a picture of my company. Every aspect of my company, including sales, production, and administration, is headed by an executive who understands our competitive advantage and consistently works to ensure it remains sustainable. I know that profits don't equal value unless the next owner can achieve at the same level. My company is built so its value will transfer without fail.

Unfortunately, the most common animal in the entrepreneurial zoo is the white elephant, not the cash cow (only 10 percent of all companies ever sell). Successful entrepreneurs are, by their nature, smart risk takers who bet right most of the time. To also become a builder, operator, or planner, you will need the right kind of tough-love advice. Valuable companies, as compared with merely profitable companies, are built to create a competitive advantage and are operated by people and processes that make that advantage bulletproof.

NOTES

NOTES

17. IS YOUR CPA MORE LIKE YOUR HISTORY TEACHER OR YOUR COACH?

A. I consider my CPA one of the necessary evils of operating a business. I assume the financial statements he prepares are accurate, as are the taxes, but beyond those commodity services, he adds zero value to my business. A couple of times we've met to discuss his ideas for improving the business. However, they were generic and unhelpful. I probably could use some help with our finances, since sales and profits are both eroding and my bookkeeper is clueless as to the cause. Deep down I don't think my CPA cares about us; he only cares about his fees.

B. My accountant is pretty sharp. She has gotten me out of a few scrapes with the IRS and my bank. Although she may have some good ideas, she's not confident enough to effectively present them or challenge me. But then again, my personality is very forceful, so maybe that's more my fault than hers. Over the years I'm afraid our relationship, like that of an older married couple, has devolved into her mostly telling me either what I want to hear or something I already know.

C.   My accountant is my principal business adviser. Not only is he a smart guy, but he's the most honest person I know. I turn to him to help resolve not only business issues but also an occasional personal one. He truly cares about me and my company. He routinely goes above and beyond. He introduced me to my attorney and banker, who are also great team members. Because my accountant deals with so many different businesses and takes the time to really understand them, his advice has helped me avoid the big mistakes. His ability to translate what he has learned from his largest clients to my business has supercharged our profitable growth. He doesn't just chronicle our history; he helps make it. Clearly, our CPA is in the running for my company's most valuable player every year. Oh yeah—he also provides great tax and accounting advice.

You may have had a crush on your high school history teacher, but it was probably your basketball coach who changed your life. Similarly, your accountant can completely change the trajectory of your business. He should be a financial coach who cares about your success so much that he will take the time to understand your business and your goals for it. He should provide on-target advice even when—or maybe especially when—you don't want to hear it. Over time, he should be helping you develop into a topflight business executive who is able to effectively lead your company, no matter how large it grows.

NOTES

NOTES

18. IS YOUR HIRING PROCESS "THE MORE, THE MERRIER" OR "THE FEW, THE PROUD"?

A.   Since we really don't have a human resources department, we usually hire the first candidate who even
marginally fits our qualifications. We figure we'll train
her up once she is on board. Honestly, this works
only when we're lucky and the candidates are honest
about their qualifications, and when they're assigned
to a talented mentor. Our success rate is well below 50
percent. Even when we land a superior candidate,
our lack of training procedures results in a protracted
spool-up time. I note problems at both ends of the employee spectrum. That is, we hire too fast and fire too
slow. Moreover, we don't present a clear path forward
for the best performers. Help!

B.   Our human resources people recruit our candidates.
They are fairly good about matching a candidate's
qualifications to the job description; however, our
on-boarding process is disorganized. How our new hires
learn to do it "our way" is ill-defined. Once the new folks
settle in and we find a champion, they do fine. However,
there is no guarantee this will occur. We bat above .500,

but not by much. We're probably weakest on our weeding-out process. Frankly, when we hire a dead horse, we switch to a bigger whip rather than having that employee advance his or her career elsewhere.

C.   We recently realized our human resources department is much better at compliance than recruiting. Recruiting is essentially a sales function, so we now have a recruiting department staffed with salespeople. We recruit continually, which gives us a large universe of candidates to choose from when we have a position to fill. We interview only those candidates whose qualifications closely match our need. Once we select a candidate, we have an extremely detailed on-boarding process, which allows new hires to quickly get up to speed. Still, we occasionally make a mistake, and when we do, we counsel out quickly, access our large candidate pool, and move forward. Since we are growing quickly and continually evaluating our people, our employees always have opportunity for advancement.

Since most businesses today are service driven, acquiring, training, and evaluating talent is likely the company's most important internal function. If you're using the technique of "the more, the merrier," you know it's time consuming and expensive. The estimated cost of a bad hire is one times that person's salary, so you should adopt the Marines' philosophy of "the few, the proud." Also, as with the military, if you want an elite force, you must reward superior performance with promotion and honorably discharge those who fail to measure up.

NOTES

NOTES

19. CAN YOU JUDGE YOUR COMPANY'S BOOK BY ITS COVER?

A. Over the years I have come to recognize what I'm best at and have built my company around it. With that said, it's difficult for me to articulate what "it" is, except that customers seem to like it. I suppose that's my unique brand. I try to communicate it to my sales force. Some get it and others have their own idea as to our competitive advantage. As long as it works for them, it is OK with me. Our lack of consistency is evidenced by our marketing efforts, which are disjointed and inconsistent in communicating our competitive advantage. Our tie doesn't match our suit and our belt doesn't match our shoes; it is a good thing we don't sell clothes.

B. After several discussions with an advertising agency, we hammered out some good brochures. In my opinion the pieces accurately set forth our value proposition and brand. Our sales force uses the brochures as an effective door opener or leave-behind. I'd say this is mostly our seasoned—that is to say, our older—sales folks. The younger sales team members are constantly complaining about our lack of a digital presence and message. I've looked at our web page and it seems OK to me. After all, we aren't Amazon.

C.   My management team and I expend significant effort maintaining what we believe is a very valuable, unique, and sustainable competitive advantage. And we are congruently building the marketing of our brand around it. As a result of my management team's many sessions with the sales and marketing departments as well as our advertising agency, we have a strong message about what our business promises to our customers. We believe a brand is a promise, and we consistently portray it across all of our communication, including print and especially digital. Our website is an easy-to-access window into exactly what makes our product unique and valuable. We believe our customers and potential customers are able to easily discern our features and benefits from the rich content on our site.

Your business's cover is probably a poor reflection of what's actually in your book. It's likely that most of your sales and marketing information has developed over time through accretion and avulsion rather than a thorough analysis of your company's promise to your customer. Instead of making selling easier by telling your customers exactly what you stand for and what they can expect, your jumbled message likely contradicts your claims or simply confuses your customers and potential customers. You must determine your competitive advantage and broadcast it with a congruent message across all of your media (and don't forget to tell everyone in your company about it too, since they are often the last to know!).

NOTES

NOTES

20. IS YOUR NEXT ROLE AS A HERO?

A.   I can't wait to be a former business owner. Like a prisoner, I'm marking off the days until I can sell. I don't have any real plans for what's next except taking my shoulder off the wheel, which sounds really good to me right now. My business is so time consuming, I have no real outside interests. I have a few retired friends who claim they miss their careers and are looking for part-time consulting work (unsuccessfully so far; it seems there are more consultants than projects). That won't be me. R & R could never be boring, and I'll be successful at retirement because I'm successful at everything I try.

B.   I am a bit ambivalent about what I would do if I sold my business today. However, I do have a few interests outside of business. I love travel, fine dining, and wine. There are also many great books I need to read. Over the years, I have vetted several charitable organizations and ultimately selected a few that are worthy. I donate money and on occasion attend events for these charities. I don't know their management teams or their board members, but I would like to get more involved when I retire. Upon reflection, I am fairly certain I will be able to fill my days productively.

C.   I am really not sure if selling my business or passing it along to my children will be the correct move. If my board and family agree it is best to sell, I will go along with that decision. We have great people and processes in place, so clearly we are ready to sell if the time is right. I will admit the toughest part will be overcoming the re-investment risk hurdle, because I believe the company will continue to grow, but I also know one can stay too long at the fair. Once liberated from the business world, I am going to take the plunge headlong into two chari-ties. I have been on both of their boards for years and they're begging me to take on a more active role (in fund-raising, of course). Giving back is very important, and I truly believe in the success-to-significance model. In ad-dition, through my trade group, I have met some young owners, whom I mentor. I will be seeing them more reg-ularly and may even join their boards. I may no longer be earning the big bucks, but I know I can add significant val-ue to society, and I can't wait to get started.

Maximizing your God-given talents outside the business arena requires significant preparation, just like everything else in your business career. Getting involved with organizations, profit or nonprofit, while you have the power base of your company is critical. If you wait until you are "that retired guy or gal" to get involved, you will be perceived as less relevant—and you most likely will be. Retirement doesn't mean disengaged; it means reengaged.

NOTES

NOTES

EVALUATION

OK, let's see how you did. Give yourself 10 points for every C answer, 5 points for every B answer, and as you may have guessed, 0 points for every A answer. If you scored 150 or more, congratulations! You own and operate a very valuable, supercharged business, and you should send me your résumé. If you scored 80–149 points, you are to be commended for adopting processes that partly uncouple the success of your business from you, but you still have work to do to truly supercharge your company. If you scored less than 80, your company's success is practically wholly dependent upon you. Your talents, your continued involvement in every aspect of your business, and most important, your ongoing desire to succeed are what's making your company successful, and you are not a sustainable resource.

As a business owner you can never rest on your laurels. There is no such thing as neutral. Either your company is moving forward or it's moving in reverse. Remember, although you may be a successful entrepreneur, if your company is overly reliant on you, your strength is your company's greatest weakness. So, address the 20 High-Performance Questions, move to C answers only, and watch your profits and value go through the roof while you blow the doors off your competition!

ABOUT THE AUTHOR

Patrick Burke, a CPA and attorney, is the managing partner of Burke & Schindler, CPAs, a firm he founded in 1984. Since the firm's inception, Burke has continuously recruited the most talented professionals to broaden the scope of the practice and to ensure Burke & Schindler clients receive top-notch service. The firm specializes in business consulting, taxation, audit and accounting, executive recruiting and staffing, and retirement plan administration.

Burke is a respected expert in business acquisitions and sales, deal structuring, value building and succession planning. In addition, he has advised more than 100 highly successful start-ups. His commitment to a proactive approach has earned him the trust and respect of his clients. He exceeds expectations by becoming clients' go-to business advisor.

Burke has been a featured lecturer on entrepreneurship at the University of Dayton and numerous seminars. He is a former member of the "Forty Under 40" business leaders in Cincinnati and a member of the Ohio Society of Certified Public Accountants, the American Institute of Certified Public Accountants, and the Ohio and American Bar Associations.

Currently, he is chairman of the board of directors of a closely held $70 million medical consulting company and board member (including chairman of the audit and compensation committees) of a closely held $500 million real estate services business and holds Series 7 and Series 63 licenses.

Burke received his J.D. from the University of Cincinnati Law School and his B.S. cum laude from the University of Dayton.

Outside of work, Patrick is active with Boys Hope Girls Hope of Cincinnati, DePaul Cristo Rey High School, and The Dynamic Catholic Institute.

If you'd like help buying a business,
running the one you have more profitably,
or selling your business for top dollar,
please contact Patrick Burke:

www.burkecpa.com
901 Adams Crossing
Cincinnati, OH 45202
513-455-8200
business@burkecpa.com